For my father, William Going . . .
his love of Frank Lloyd Wright's art and his passion for
the natural world inspired this book, and his integrity inspires my life
—K. L. G.

For everyone who contributes to keeping the beauty
and shape of our world alive—and for M., R. & M., and C.
—L. S.

And special thanks to Keiran Murphy, a historian with the Taliesin Preservation
who listened to my questions and offered answers along the way.—L. S.

BEACH LANE BOOKS ▪ An imprint of Simon & Schuster Children's Publishing Division ▪ 1230 Avenue of the Americas, New York, New York 10020 ▪ Text copyright © 2017 by K. L. Going ▪ Illustrations copyright © 2017 by Lauren Stringer ▪ All rights reserved, including the right of reproduction in whole or in part in any form. ▪ Beach Lane Books is a trademark of Simon & Schuster, Inc. ▪ For information about special discounts for bulk purchases, please contact Simon & Schuster Special Sales at 1-866-506-1949 or business@simonandschuster.com. ▪ The Simon & Schuster Speakers Bureau can bring authors to your live event. For more information or to book an event, contact the Simon & Schuster Speakers Bureau at 1-866-248-3049 or visit our website at www.simonspeakers.com. ▪ Book design by Lauren Stringer and Lauren Rille ▪ The text for this book was set in P22 Eaglefeather. ▪ The illustrations for this book were rendered in acrylic, gouache, watercolor, and colored pencil on Arches oil paper. ▪ The quote on page 56 is from page 26 of An Autobiography by Frank Lloyd Wright. ▪ Manufactured in China ▪ 0923 SCP ▪ 10 9 8 7 6 ▪ Library of Congress Cataloging-in-Publication Data ▪ Names: Going, K. L. (Kelly L.), author. | Stringer, Lauren, illustrator. ▪ Title: The shape of the world : a portrait of Frank Lloyd Wright / K.L. Going ; illustrated by Lauren Stringer. ▪ Description: New York : Beach Lane Books, 2017. | Includes bibliographical references. | Audience: Ages 5-10. | Audience: K to Grade 5. ▪ Identifiers: LCCN 2017001386| ISBN 9781442478213 (hardback) | ISBN 9781442478282 (e-book) ▪ Subjects: LCSH: Wright, Frank Lloyd, 1867-1959—Juvenile literature. | Architects—United States—Biography—Juvenile literature. | BISAC: JUVENILE NONFICTION / Biography & Autobiography / Art. | JUVENILE NONFICTION / Architecture. | JUVENILE NONFICTION / Concepts / Size & Shape. ▪ Classification: LCC NA737.W7 G65 2017 | DDC 720.92 [b] —dc23 LC record available at https://lccn.loc.gov/2017001386

K. L. Going

Lauren Stringer

THE SHAPE OF THE WORLD

A Portrait of Frank Lloyd Wright

∎∎∎

BEACH LANE BOOKS ∎ New York   London   Toronto   Sydney   New Delhi

One night, a momma rocked
a baby in an old wooden chair.
"Someday," she whispered,
"you will build beautiful buildings."

The baby smiled and cooed.
He did not know about beautiful buildings.
He hadn't seen soaring skyscrapers
or elegant museums.
But someday he would learn.

When the baby grew into a boy,
his mother gave him gifts:
cubes, spheres, cones, pyramids, cylinders.
The boy loved the smooth shapes.
They felt soft against his fingers
and heavy in his palm.

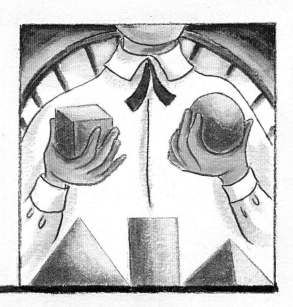

It was fun to build them up
and knock them down.
He loved to stack them
this way and that,
that way and this.
They could grow
tall or wide,
flat or round.

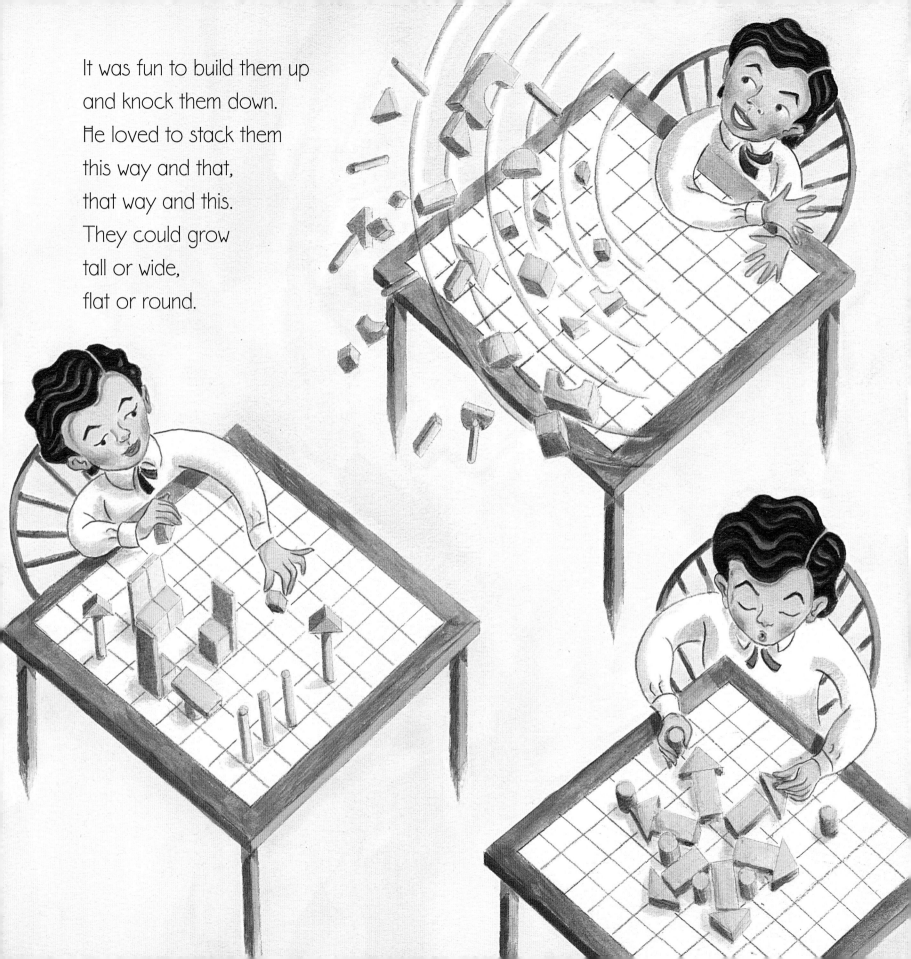

AH-HA!

The boy had learned a secret.
Every shape was many shapes.

When he was older, the boy spent
each summer on his uncle's farm.
He worked hard from
sunrise to sunset,
but sometimes . . .
when no one was looking . . .

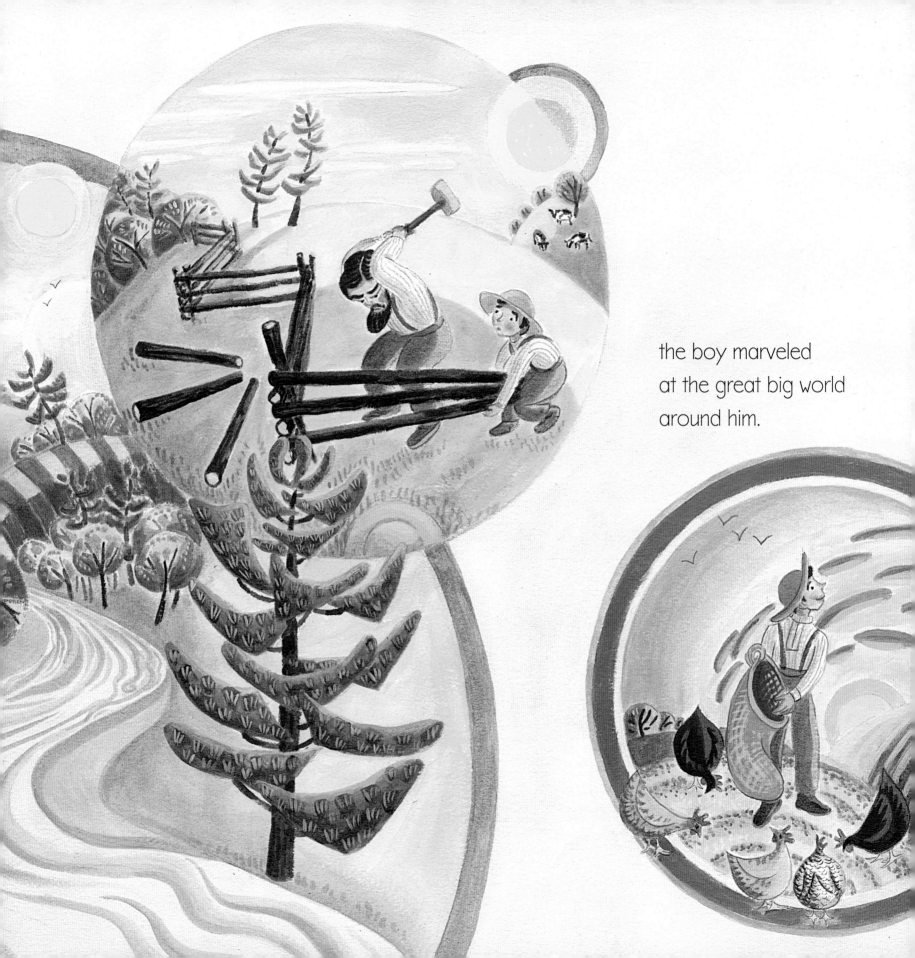

the boy marveled
at the great big world
around him.

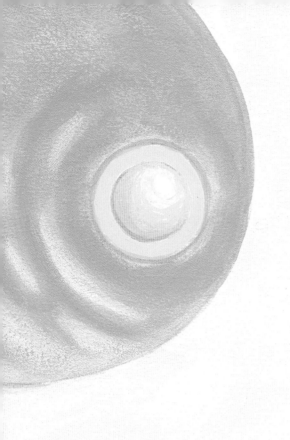

He saw shapes everywhere he looked.
He found an arch in the pathway of a frog,
a cone inside the petals of a flower,
a triangle in a spider's web,
pyramid peaks of anthills,
and perfect hexagons in
an empty piece of honeycomb.

He saw the shiny sphere of the sun,
and the glowing circle moon.

Sometimes the boy hid in the tall grass,
watching the weeds bend and sway,
studying the shape of a bird's flight.

He asked himself many questions.
Did the sky have a shape?
How many shapes were hidden in a tree?

Raindrops made changing shapes—clear and cold.

Lightning made jagged shapes—sharp and burnt.

The river made smooth shapes—long and curved.

The boy loved the shape of the world.
He wanted to build buildings
as amazing as the world around him.

When the boy grew into a man, he became an architect. He worked hard from sunrise to sunset, but he never forgot the smooth weight of the blocks his mother had given him when he was a boy. He remembered the hills and prairies surrounding his family's farm.

When other architects chose walls,
he chose windows.

When others set their buildings apart,
his were one with the world around them.

He built a house
like a honeycomb,

a museum like a shell,

and towers as tall and thick as trees.

People from far and wide came to see his work.
When they looked at his buildings,
they imagined the rolling
landscape of hills, and felt
the wide expanse of sky
surround them.

Like the boy, they too learned
to love the shape of the world.

One night, when the architect was an old man,
he rocked back and forth
in his mother's wooden chair.
Her promise had come true.

When he was a baby,
he had not known about
beautiful buildings.
He hadn't seen soaring
skyscrapers or elegant museums,
but he had learned.

Someday had come and gone . . .

and he had changed
the shape of the world.

AUTHOR'S NOTE ■ *The Shape of the World* is based on the life and work of Frank Lloyd Wright, who was born on June 8, 1867, and died on April 9, 1959. Wright has been called America's greatest architect. He built beautiful buildings in a style that was both elegant and unique. Frank credited his mother for introducing him to his calling while he was still a baby. She put up pictures of cathedrals in his nursery, and when he was old enough, she gave him a set of Froebel Gifts—simple geometrical blocks that he used to build buildings and towers.

He said that the blocks taught him every shape was many shapes, and that even when he grew up, he could still feel the blocks in his fingers. Frank was also greatly influenced by nature. As a child, he spent summers working on his family's farm and studying the prairies of Wisconsin. This love of nature shows in every building he designed. He once said, "No house should ever be *on* a hill or *on* anything. It should be *of* the hill. Belonging to it. Hill and house should live together each the happier for the other."

ILLUSTRATOR'S NOTE ■ My research for this book began while on an artist's retreat in Spring Green, Wisconsin, the location of Taliesin, where Frank Lloyd Wright worked on his family's farm as a youth and lived and designed for most of his adult life. I hiked the grounds, photographing trees, sky, hills, birds, lakes, the river, wildflowers, and buildings. When I took the tour offered by the Taliesin Preservation through the interiors of Wright's house and the Fellowship studios, my appreciation for how nature can inspire architecture and design was transformed. After visiting Taliesin, I visited my local library. Wright designed more than 1,000 structures and completed 500 works, so I had no shortage of beautifully illustrated books to pore through.

His drawings of buildings, windows, and rugs influenced how I composed each illustration in this book. I learned to use the tools of a twentieth-century architect—rulers, triangles, and a compass—in order to convey what I found most inspiring from my investigations into his life and works. The illustrations were painted with an earthy color palette to reflect Wright's philosophy of "organic architecture"—a belief in designing structures that are in harmony with their environment. And the square format of this book echoes Wright's signature: the red square, a symbol that may owe its origin to his love of Japanese prints but was also inspired by the red lilies that grew wild on the family farm. "The spot of red made by a lily on the green always gave him an emotion."

■ ■ ■

SOURCES

Adkins, Jan. *Frank Lloyd Wright, a Twentieth-Century Life.* Up Close. New York: Viking, 2007.

Fleming, Diane Bresnan. *Simply Wright: A Journey into the Ideas of Frank Lloyd Wright's Architecture.* Madison, WI: Castleconal Press, 2004.

Heinz, Thomas A. *Frank Lloyd Wright Glass Art.* London: Academy Group LTD, 1994.

Hess, Alan, and Alan Weintraub. *Frank Lloyd Wright: The Buildings.* New York: Rizzoli, 2008.

———. *Frank Lloyd Wright: The Houses.* New York: Rizzoli, 2005.

Pfeiffer, Bruce Brooks. *Frank Lloyd Wright Designs: The Sketches, Plans, and Drawings.* New York: Rizzoli, 2011.

Pfeiffer, Bruce Brooks; and David Larkin. *Frank Lloyd Wright: The Masterworks.* New York: Rizzoli, 1993.

Thorne-Thomsen, Kathleen. *Frank Lloyd Wright for Kids: His Life and Ideas.* Chicago: Chicago Review Press, 2014.

Wright, Frank Lloyd. *An Autobiography.* 2nd ed. New York: Duell, Sloan and Pearce, 1943.

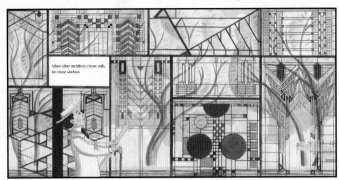

Clockwise from top left:

Bradley House, Kankakee, IL, ca. 1900

Ennis House, Los Angeles, CA, ca. 1924

Barnsdall House (Hollyhock House), Los Angeles, CA, ca. 1921

Glasner House, Glencoe, IL, ca. 1905

Dana House, Springfield, IL, ca. 1903

Coonley Playhouse, Riverside, IL, ca. 1912

Willits House, Highland Park, IL, ca. 1901

Martin House, Buffalo, NY, ca. 1904

Robie House, Chicago, IL, ca. 1908–1910

■ ■ ■

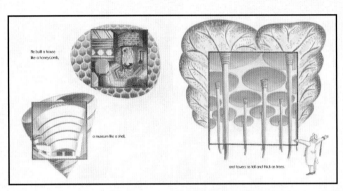

Kaufmann Residence (Fallingwater), Mill Run, PA, ca. 1935

■ ■ ■

Solomon R. Guggenheim Museum, New York, NY, ca. 1959

Hanna House (Honeycomb House), Stanford, CA, ca. 1937

Johnson Wax Headquarters, Racine, WI, ca. 1939

■ ■ ■

Clockwise from top left:

Solomon R. Guggenheim Museum, New York, NY, ca. 1959

Taliesin, Spring Green, WI, ca. 1911–1959

Heurtley House, Oak Park, IL, ca. 1902

Barnsdall House (Hollyhock House), Los Angeles, CA, ca. 1921

Frank Lloyd Wright Home and Studio, Oak Park, IL, ca. 1889

■ ■ ■

In the stars, clockwise from top left:

Taliesin West, Scottsdale, AR, ca. 1937

Dana House, Springfield, IL, ca. 1903

Solomon R. Guggenheim Museum, New York, NY, ca. 1959

Pope-Leighey House (Usonian house), near Alexandria, VA, ca. 1941

Unitarian Meeting House, Madison, WI, ca. 1949–1951

Price Tower, Bartlesville, OK, ca. 1952–1956

On the land, left to right:

Midway Barn at Taliesin, Spring Green, WI, ca. 1938–1947

Romeo and Juliet Windmill Tower at Taliesin, Spring Green, WI, ca. 1897